Auntie Jodi's
Helpful Hints

Ginger Jam Media
Los Angeles, California

auntiejodi.com

ISBN: 978-0-9907276-1-3

Auntie Jodi's Helpful Hints

Jodi Adler

Ginger Jam Media
Los Angeles

To Mom and Dad—and to my readers.

Table of Contents

SPRING

1

When someone asks your sign, just make it up—and, yes, they will tell you how much you are like your fictional sign. That's just one of the ways I amuse myself when attending a soirée. Today I am a Taurus.

2

Do you have an overbooking, neurotic socialite/poseur pestering you for a luncheon date—but only if you rearrange your life to meet her tightly ordered one-hour window of opportunity? Have an iron-clad agenda of your own, and wage a one-on-one battle of schedules. Always remember to use terms such as *life coach, banker, parole officer*, or *Pilates instructor*, so the importance of your schedule always trumps those trifling conflicts in her petty little life.

3

Getting wedding or coming-of-age party invitations from people you haven't seen in many years? Just because you have a reputation as a great gift-giver, you should not get cynical about the reason for this reconnection. Attend, and make a donation to a controversial non-PC cause dear to your heart—the greater the controversy, the greater your chance of not having to worry about another gift-begging invite from this long-lost lackey.

4

Awkward with introductions?
Go for the two-cheek air kiss
when meeting someone new.
Do not ever actually plant your
lips on anyone's face—that is an
obvious sign of a rank amateur.
You can tell them you picked
up the habit from a friend who
summered on the Continent.
Speak in a thick French or
Italian accent. Ciao, baby.

5

Find yourself in conversation
with pretentious poseurs?
Simply exclaim, "Sassy!" or
"You go, Girl!" This allows you
to gracefully exit, as it interrupts
their convoluted train of
thought.

6

This works exceptionally well if
there is an "Upstairs,

Downstairs" or "Downton Abbey" situation in the hosts' home: Instead of mingling, find a way into the kitchen, and offer to help the help. Don't talk, just listen . . . chances are, you will learn oodles about your hosts. This newfound information will help you with small talk (and blackmail) in the future.

7

Can't get enough of holidays like International Coffee Day, Sweetest Day, or National Mustard Day? Create your own special day. Refrain from going to work, and petition the local legislature to acknowledge your specialness. Let's call tomorrow National Sleeping It Off Day, next Monday International Estheticians' Day . . . and don't forget every dance-lover's favorite, Cha-Cha Thursday (I think that'll be in March).

8

Feeling nauseated about the April 15th day of government thievery? Whether your funds are earned or inherited, remember that all of us payers are somewhat distraught. We would never get political, and do not have the necessary licenses to advise about being overtaxed . . . we always rely upon our CPA, our business manager, and Glenfiddich.

9

Watching a parade? Why not dress in the anticipated style of your favorite float or band? Remember—there will probably be some type of queen involved, so tiaras and feathers are your go-to accessories. If you happen to be a drill team or marching band alum, you are expected to point out the off-the-beat, out-of-line steppers.

10

Driver/chauffeur have the day off? When swerving to avoid rear-ending the texting driver in front of you, always smile and wave while you drive alongside this texting maniac. As you pass, use discretion when determining the number of fingers to use as you wave.

11

Have you been told it's rude to disagree? Here is a polite way around that silly rule: If you should find yourself in conversation with a dolt, wait for an opportune time to remark, "That's a macro issue; I'm speaking on a micro level," or vice-versa. This generally stops them in their tracks, and gives you a chance to politely shut the fools down. Manners do count.

12

Has someone who is suffering
from Excessive Hugging
Syndrome invaded your space
one time too many? Combat
those overhuggers and
boobsquishers by turning your
body ninety degrees as the
hugger lunges toward you.
Speedy reflexes and practice will
you help perfect this technique.
If all else fails, remember to
reach quickly for your shiv.

13

Have you received an invitation
to some sort of ghastly reunion?
The only reasons to go are to
show everyone how fabulous
you look, because you have a
prestigious career, or if you've
become incredibly rich. Even
if you are remarkably un-
accomplished, you are certainly
welcome to attend, but make
sure you wear a pair of dark
sunglasses at all times. And—

13

this is fun—immediately tell all attendees that they haven't changed a bit; it makes for unique conversation starters. It is only after you've been chatting up another attendee a bit that you need to politely inquire as to his or her name.

14

If the butler has the night off, and you're racing through the grocer's looking for the perfect tin of caviar—don't forget, the rules of the road must be applied when pushing your cart. Move to the right, signal lane changes, and never text while trying to negotiate your way around the pre-cut crudités. Someone cut you off in aisle three? Not to worry—help them have more fun at checkout. Just drop a few extra items into their cart when no one's looking. Alcohol, deodorant, or perhaps a rump roast: these are some of my favorite "toss-and-run" items.

15

Feeling as if you have lost your raison d'être? Just grab a clipboard and head out into the world. You will immediately be granted entry into all sorts of fun places. If anyone should start asking you probing questions, start taking notes as you give vague responses. Wearing a jaunty hat will lend you that extra flair.

16

At a meet-and-greet, but not feeling too meety or greety? Take out a pen, and offer to sign the programs, menus, or napkins. No, you do not have to use your real name, and it is best if the signature is illegible. If anyone asks, wink and tell them you are a writer.

17

Have you been sneered at for using the phrase, "THE wife" (or "THE hubby")? Why not have a giggle at tonight's gathering by substituting a number in place of "the." Watch jaws drop when you say, "my first wife…" This is hugely amusing if you are still on your first marriage.

18

Feel like giving that fake compliment-giver a smack in her fake-talking mouth? Remember to always be gracious, say "thank you," and reciprocate as soon as possible. Why not have a sincere retort at the ready? Something along the lines of, "You look ever so much better since your surgery" always works well.

19

Heading to an award ceremony? Looking good takes careful planning. Make sure all Botox touch-ups are completed at least three weeks before you stroll down the red carpet. Four weeks . . . and you'll be a photog's dream.

20

Carry a pack of sticky notes with you, so you can leave short helpful hints of your own in strategic places. Hosts' kitchen a bit sloppy? Use the county health department code to rate the site. When leaving your letter critique (A, B, or C), always remember to use good penmanship.

21

Keep using those sticky notes. Does the car next to you need some parking help? Put a Post-It with your ever-so-thoughtful suggestions on their windshield, and of course, be polite. Spelling counts.

22

Here's a way to subtly show off your new tatt. Oh wait, there is no way to be subtle with a new tattoo . . . just strategically shred a T-shirt so it highlights your inky creation. While at the gym, you won't have to wait long as your friends gaze/gawk/gander at the brilliance of your ink and at your obvious intellectual prowess.

23

Using words with double meanings is a sure-fire hit at a party. Amuse yourself by mentioning to your party mates that your tranny is on the fritz. Whether the gathering features

car lovers or cross-dressers,
you will quickly make loads
of new friends.

24

Never let a grudge go to waste.
The key with grudges is to
pretend you have "moved on,"
while plotting your revenge.
When you finally get to zing,
prank, or kill your victim, no
one will ever suspect you are the
evil mastermind.

25

Need to lose weight in a hurry
for that red carpet photo-op
next week? Simply contract a
case of food poisoning, and
boom—twelve pounds will be
gone in only three days. Not
only is it fast and easy—the best
part is that there are no silly
books to buy, food to measure,
or rules to follow.

26

Feeling a bit ignored during award season? Put on your best evening attire, and head to a local movie theater. Position yourself at the entrance and thank all the folks for coming out to see you. Remember to bring along a mini bottle of hand sanitizer—thanking all of the "little people" can be a very germy business.

27

Conversation at a lull while you are at a formal dinner? Convince your table mates to do "the wave" whenever the help enters with another course. While sipping sherry and nibbling on a petit macaroon, keep the fun going by pulling out an inflatable beach ball to volley around.

28

In a meeting-from-hell? Use
one of those clown lapel flowers
that squirt water, and keep
things lively by aiming for
specific body parts of other
attendees. Keep score, hits v.
misses . . . you will be surprised
at how much fun meetings
become and how quickly you
get the attention of Human
Resources.

29

While chatting at a cocktail
party, should you find yourself
staring at a painting that is
hanging at a not-quite-right
angle, divulge to a few that
you've recently become feng
shui-certified. Watch the
excitement mount as you direct
your fellow party-going minions
to adjust the listing artwork.
When you are finished,
encourage the crowd to inhale

deeply, and admire the room's improved energy flow.

30

When dealing with children, be they yours or others', you must include the slow head turn and look of disdain in your repertoire of reactions. If this does not immediately work, I suggest immediately lacing the parent's and child's milk or juice with an 80-proof spirit.

31

Handholding and career counseling can be so much fun. The next time you spend hours on the phone with your stuck-in-a-rut pal, send a little note of encouragement with a neatly typed invoice for your session fee tucked inside. You probably won't get paid, but they probably won't complain (or talk) to you again. It becomes a real-life win-win situation.

32

When posing for a photo with a chatty and adoring fan, concentrate on the camera, not the dear fan's conversation. A good photo lasts forever . . . and the fan can always be cropped out at a later date.

33

Those darling little children of yours down with the flu? Simply go on an impromptu vacay with your hubby . . . by the time you come back, the kiddies will be healthy as can be.

34

When dealing with an over-manscaped Lothario who salaciously sends you unwelcome winks to make his

oh-so-subtle points, simply
wink back, and ask about his
favorite esthetician. Sharing
notes about skincare sends
any hints of his remaining
testosterone out the proverbial
window.

35

When asked a question, always
have an answer at the ready.
This works for politicians, and
it will work easily for you. It
doesn't matter if your response
is reality-based. Be definite
about your point of view, and
you will be surprised at how
many minions automatically line
up to agree with you.

36

If you should be asked to get on
a scale while sashaying through
a doctor's office, tell the darling
doctor that you are concerned
about getting too thin, so you

need to pass on this glorious offer. Remember, the only large numbers you should ever worry about are the ones listed in a pre-nup, or as karats.

37

If an over-solicitous kumbaya type shares that you seem "angry," simply laugh and tell the poor soul "it's called 'having an opinion.'"

38

Auntie Jodi would like to tell you that if you ever dare to give up, don't bother to call and complain about it—it's just too dull, my darlings . . . but if you really must complain, make sure it's about something important, like a shortage of champagne or the government's ban on foie gras.

SUMMER

39

Drooling yourself awake on your party hosts' Victorian chaise? Quickly endear yourself to your host by taking artful snapshots of other still-slumbering partygoers. When leaving, remember to graciously thank your hosts for their hospitality, while gently reminding them that you have the shots digitally saved to your cloud or home hard drive. Thinking ahead like this is an invaluable skill, especially if you are faced with the unkind threat of a lawsuit.

40

Need to lose a few pounds, so you can slither down the red carpet in your Atelier Privé gown? Prevent diet derangement by swapping your evening fruit allotment for a glass of Cristal, cabernet, or chardonnay. Fruit is fruit, n'est-ce pas?

41

Nonjudgmental type condescendingly tell you that they "don't judge"? Take your pal to the beach, and just for fun do your best Dancing with the Stars/Olympic judge impersonation—hold up colorful 3x5 cards (boldly numbered from 1 to 10) as swimsuit-clad sun worshipers amble on by.

42

Having a hard time suffering
fools today? Answer all
questions as tersely as possible.
Remove all humor, wit, and
sarcasm from your retorts. They
still won't get it, but you'll be
elated at how the befuddled
soul makes for an even better
foil. *En garde!*

43

Is a manner-less buffoon asking
overly nosy questions? Make
good use of the non sequitur:
"Q. How old are you? A. 34D."
"Q. What was your net income
last year? A. Tampons." "Q.
You're not married? A.
Ecclesiastes 3:7, or Proverbs
10:19." Always remember to
flash a sincere smile when
responding.

44

Dealing with an alleged business pro who uses happy-face emoticons when corresponding? Cut through the smiley stuff by ending your notes with non-smiley statements such as, "My cat died," or "Today's the tenth anniversary of my grandfather's death." Expect to receive a frownie face back in the response.

45

If an open-minded free thinker says something along the lines of, "she doesn't even look Jewish/black/Mexican/etc." make her actually try to think by simply responding, "like me?" Alternately, "describe what that looks like." Watch as squirming and backpedaling ensue.

46

Daylight savings time ruining your style? Set up your own personal time zones—perhaps one for each room in your villa—and let the world reset itself to you.

47

Auntie Jodi knows you are proud of yourself, but sometimes, just sometimes . . . you may want to rethink that chest thumping. It sounds as if you're bragging. Perhaps it might be better to just let us accidentally find out how wonderful you are. The art of being subtle is so sorely missed these days.

48

Is the over-coiffed theatre patron sitting in the box next to you wearing enough cloyingly sweet, heady, or floral cologne to entice the EPA into yet another government-funded pollution study? Come prepared with color-coordinated surgical masks. Imploringly—and loudly—ask your date or spouse to tie your mask on for you. Remember to reciprocate with him or her later—in the theater or at home.

49

Is a dear one hinting for a bit of flattery about a new item of clothing, haircut, or accessory that is simply hideous and beyond ugly? Respond to that needy plea with the phrase, "That's so you!" Voilà—the dear one's Neanderthal tastes are not called into question. For fun, you might take a photo so the look can be submitted to a fashion-disaster-fixer or makeover columnist.

50

Spy someone's designer label hanging out the back of their collar? Your response on this one depends on your relationship with the label dangler. Do you like him or her? Discreetly position yourself close enough to whisper a warning, and possibly help with the tuck-in. Not a fan? Ignore the dangling label; it's probably a knock-off jacket anyway.

51

Auntie Jodi would like to suggest that the DMV expand to cover texting pedestrians. That way, those of us caught behind someone who is not able to simultaneously walk and text will no longer have to avoid the dear one who has stopped in his/her tracks to thumb at his or her phone. Perhaps phones should come with an app that automatically flashes a white brake light behind all stalled-out texters. A blinking turn signal might also come in handy.

52

Should you be asked out by someone who is blissfully unaware of your lack of interest, feign hurt and shock as you respond, "Darling, we went out to dinner four years ago." Raise one eyebrow, slowly shake your head, or simply sigh as you sashay away.

53

Planning a party, and trying to take the fashionably late friends' habits into account? Counter their tardiness by sending out invitations with staggered start times. Take bets with the help about who will actually show up before the flambé goes cold.

54

Have a few pals who double-book themselves so that their positive R.S.V.P. actually means "I'll work the room for ten minutes, then escape to a VIP party"? Entice them to stay by holding a carnival-style raffle at your next soirée, handing out tickets upon guests' arrival. Wait until after dessert to announce the winning number, and make the grand prize worthwhile—perhaps that little investment cottage that is now an underwater fixer-upper.

55

Auntie Jodi is thrilled to be getting all of these fabulous invitations to online events. Her dance card is absolutely overflowing. If only she actually knew the kind people who were so graciously inviting her to join in the festivities. It might be even more exciting if she were interested in all the darling little details of your life.

56

Feeling as if you are not doing your part for the community? Simply offer to mentor a needy soul. It does not matter what the topic; you will be surprised at how any and all guidance is welcomed. Common-sense advice is best—especially for the dears with those pesky profound questions.

57

Know someone who always needs to have the last word? Shut down this neurotic know-it-all with sing-song phrases such as, "told ya so," or the always popular tiff-ender, "are not, are too." If this still does not work, then stick out your tongue and say "Nah nah nah nah NAH nah."

58

Overwhelmed, piqued, or dismayed by calls and messages from people you have never met or never want to chat with again? Devise a personal "do not call list," using criteria such as needy, soul-sucking, or not able to understand your humor, and **voilà**—you earn back hours, if not days, of freedom from their phone tyranny. Now go bless the genius who invented caller ID.

59

Once in a while, swap your responses to those front-porch proselytizers with those for your candidate-canvassers.

60

Forget someone's name while making an introduction at a party, inauguration, or symposium? Simply call the unknown person by the first name that pops into your empty head . . . and watch how quickly you are corrected. Kindly tell this dear soul that they might think about changing their name to the new one—for an improved numerology frequency.

61

If you are lucky enough to have possession of a business card or means of contacting Auntie Jodi, this certainly does not give you license to add that email address to your hideously boring daily newsletter. Auntie does not give a whit about your next gig or seminar, nor about your political, sexual, or philosophical orientation. Or about how you plan to market yourself into the next tax bracket. Auntie's card does not belong on the email equivalent of the "win a free lunch" fishbowl at TGIFriday's.

62

See an out-of-control wild child being ignored by overly indulgent, talking, texting, emotionally needy parents in public? When the sweet little dervish comes begging for your attention, ply him with sugar, caffeine, or alcohol before sending him or her back to Mommy. It may take a village—but darling, we are not even in the same tribe.

63

Find yourself embroiled in a deliciously dull conversation at yet another art opening, wedding, or state dinner? Make sure you know a few phrases in an obscure tongue: it is so much more polite and erudite to insult someone when language is an issue. Remember to smile knowingly while nodding your head when exiting from the somnambulant clique.

64

Networking with a group that is obviously not of a similar mind-set? Always make sure the name written on your sticky nametag is legible. No need to use your given name; an alias, nom de guerre, or stage name always makes an early exit less stressful—and greatly diminishes the odds of being tracked down by anyone in the organization.

65

Auntie Jodi does not believe in "frenemies." You are either my friend or you are not my friend. She ardently believes that she does not belong in the same atelier as those frenemy people.

Let's just call those loathsome creatures manipulative losers, and be done with them.

66

Don't ever think that your childhood years playing Monopoly, chess or Jacob's Ladder were a waste of time. Life skills—such as wealth accumulation, outsmarting your boss, or using rope to trip or strangle a pathologically evil acquaintance—will always be of value. That and target practice at your favorite shooting range.

67

Cacophonous music blaring from the not-so-trendy poseur's open car window? Wave politely and ask the driver the name of the performer, station, or podcast from which the noise is emanating. Suggest your own obscure Latin chart toppers—

"Te sunt stultus" or "Mordebit
me" as you motor away.

68

When faced with overly prying,
intrusive, or meddling queries,
simply respond with the evil
eye, a raised eyebrow, or a blank
stare. Then turn and sashay
away. Not only does this give
Access Hollywood, *National
Enquirer*, *TMZ*, and *People
Magazine* poseur snoops a
reason to pause—and possibly
think—it also makes for a great
cover shot.

69

Feeling sad, old, or in need of a
facelift because of an upcoming
birthday, anniversary, or
renegotiation meeting? Use the
ignorance of teenagers to your
advantage, and ask a few to
guess your age. Most of their
responses will top out at 35

(yes, we know that they
naively think mid-thirties is
old). Nothing feels as good
as being told you look years
younger than you really are.
Just this once, do not consider
the source.

70

Surrounded by petty nitpickers?
The next time one of them
dares to point out an endearing
minor flaw, explain that your
life is a macro project, and those
micro issues are for micro-
thinkers. Before smiling and
gracefully exiting, mention your
efforts in helping to increase the
money supply, and note that
scarce resources—like your
time—must always be properly
allocated.

71

Auntie Jodi wants to remind
you of the power of the phrase,

"I don't know." Not only does using it stop a modern-day inquisition, it also allows you to continue with your tea/coffee/vodka-tasting party duties. Also helpful: "I do not have a clue," and "I plead the Fifth." It is always best if any of these phases is uttered with absolute, solemn sincerity.

72

When offering to play matchmaker for Auntie, please remember that it is best if the suitor hails from nearly the same generation, speaks the same language, and has the ability to laugh himself silly. Having the same type of hair does *not* count, even if he does add highlights to his base color.

73

Is an absent-minded friend constantly misplacing her

glasses, keys, bracelet, or rings while visiting? Make the hunt for the lost items part of a game of Hide and Seek. If you should find the item before your pal, quickly assess its Antiques Roadshow auction value before handing it over.

74

Things rocky on the marital front? Keep a personal log of complaints, but never air them publically. Do not discuss your pet peeves, likes, dislikes—we all know that no long-term change ever really occurs. The only reason to go for marriage counseling is if you want a divorce. Auntie knows that the best marriage counselor is an ironclad pre-nup.

75

If a surly clerk is giving you below-par service, remember to always treat those who work for you with respect—the quickest way to counter a bad attitude is to incredulously, yet kindly, mirror back their words, but with your own spin. If you've been told that "I'm going to go out of my way for you," immediately and calmly repeat back, "you're going out of your way for me, Dear?" Then just stare at the clerk's nametag as you watch squirming ensue.

76

Unfamiliar soul using overly sarcastic, friendly, or fake phrases such as, "dear, hon/honey, or sweetie" when addressing you? Immediately echo back the fake endearment each time the word is tossed your way, and watch how quickly the dolt wakes up. Make sure you use the same dismissive intonation when repeating the phony terms—a sucker punch is much more

easily administered with a
heartfelt and sincere smile.

77

Auntie Jodi wishes all a joyous
Happy Canada day this July 1st,
and suggests that we in the USA
celebrate by adding an extra u to
any words with an o in them...
nouw you are an honourary
Canadian. Louve youu!

78

Worried about singeing off your
eyelashes with some not-so-
safe-and-sane fireworks?
Remember: all types of
sparklers are *de rigueur* for any
type of celebration, especially
when we are talking about our
independence, liberty, and
freedom. Auntie does love it
when the sky crackles with July
4th festivities—and when her
beau presents her with a new
sparkly, celebratory bauble.

79

When you're dating, going over the top is a spectacular thing: compliments, words of love, and the intriguing wink are all quite lovely. But going over the top before you've even met someone is . . . dare I say it . . . off-putting and scary. How do you know that someone is truly wonderful, gorgeous, witty, handsome, smart, and funny until the two of you have actually met?

80

Auntie Jodi knows your child is the most adorable creature to have ever been born—but tantrums at restaurants and screaming fits at department stores are, in reality, not so cute. Perhaps Mummy and Papa are the ones who need some home training—saying "no" early on might just prevent you from spawning yet another generation

of the overly and unjustly
entitled brat-child-parent cycle.

81

Auntie wants you to know that
lying, cheating, or stealing is
never acceptable. If you steal
her hints, her trinkets, or
anything else of tangible or
intangible value, you will be
found—not just by Auntie's
attorneys, but also, potentially,
by Auntie herself. Attorneys file
papers and work within the law;
Auntie does not.

82

Auntie understands sarcasm,
but when meeting someone for
the first time you may want to
hold off on showing off all your
über-dry wit. Dullards might
think you are mean, lovelorn
dates could see you as a threat,
and employers are likely to
immediately pull out the

company handbook. Of course, all bets are off if you have encountered an equal—so go ahead and let the repartee begin. Just be careful that the quick-witted one is not covering for some childhood issues— unless you too are in denial.

83

When faced with too much to do, simply think of all your work as empire-building. I am currently building my own empire. I am, of course, Empress Jodi, but I also like the sound of Czarina Zhodee, and HRH Jodi I. When creating your fantasy world, never let facts weigh you down.

84

Go through your list of friends every so often, and reassess that once-so-special connection. Is an old pal now living under an

assumed name? Perhaps it's
time to assume that sharing any
information with this dear one
needs to be halted. Off-kilter
funny buddy now forgetting to
take his meds? It's time to say,
"Kiss-kiss, bye-bye." Keep
your sanity by tossing away your
old save-a-soul self. The soul
you save this time might just be
your own.

85

Too many people with too
many problems trying to suck
some of your happy spirit away?
Turn on your inner "who
cares?" switch, and readjust
your personal settings.
Whenever someone over-shares
yet another tidbit from the inner
workings of his or her life, stare
. . . then smile, and reset. Keep
silently repeating this mantra:
"Who cares. Go away." Uttering
the phrase aloud helps speed up
the "go away" part of the
process, of course.

86

Having a hard time dealing with phonies, liars, cheaters, and their kind? Throw caution to the wind, and dare to tell them the truth. They probably won't believe anything you say . . . and that, my darlings, is a bit of gold. Continue by telling the pretty little liar that she's not only talented, but is also on her way to winning some kind of industry statuette.

FALL

87

Overzealous party-goers snapping unauthorized candid photos with their new cameras, phones, or gadgets? Corral those amateur paparazzi by whipping out your camera to fight fire with fire. Make sure your shots of them are as unflattering as possible . . . extortion can be so much fun.

88

Out-of-balance friend offering up unsolicited suggestions about harmonizing your energy fields? Avoid an unnecessary chakra alignment by offering her some balancing suggestions of your own that involve assets/liabilities and profit/loss statements. Chances are this dear friend is math-phobic, so watch as the energy quickly shifts to meditating (or medicating and Merlot) during your accounting recitation. This is known as a perfectly balanced case of two birds/one stone.

89

You do know that Auntie is all about good health, and there's got to be a study about coffee and red wine being healthier than a green leaf slurry. But darlings, a true size 6 is *not* obese. And cutting—then sewing—a size 9 tag back into your collar, upside-down, is just wrong. If anyone is looking at your size tag when your clothes are off, Auntie suggests putting the outfit right back on—this is obviously a prime candidate for a shopping partner, not a romantic one.

90

Amateur manipulator trying to pull your strings? Remember that the puppeteer is just a coward hiding behind the marionette. The next time she tries something clumsily sly, you'll want to discreetly mention that you have been trained in the ancient martial art of "Nocandoo." As you exit, demonstrate your kicking combination skills. *Hyah!*

91

Having murderous thoughts because an evil hater refuses to

delete a photo that portrays you in a less-than-positive light? Simply pretend you are Charlize Theron, after three hours in makeup, portraying a vagrant serial killer. Then go shoot the hater (with a camera, of course).

92

If friends with children simply do not understand the idea of an evening out without their precious offspring, no need to fret. Instead of having a kids' table, start a new trend and have a kids' restaurant and an adults' restaurant. Anyone who needs clarification can simply change guest lists.

93

Obsessing about a betrayal while alleged friends advise you to "let it go"—all while the annoying and betraying behavior grows? Let *them* go.

Let them go from your friends list, your contacts list, your dinner guest list, and your gift list. If you should ever be asked about the lost connection, just say "let it go."

94

Forced to associate with pretentious folk who have a veneer of strength, exhibit true lack of self-esteem, and have oodles of brazenly apparent ulterior motives? Give them some sincere feedback or words of gratitude or praise, and watch how fast they make a real-life U-turn.

95

Guest list growing, with a seemingly short supply of gift-bag giveaways? Start a personal swag brand. Uncap a permanent marker, and autograph some stashed-away T-shirts. You will not only be giving each guest a personalized party gift, you will also be recycling those lovely cotton blend shirts. Who says you have to be an earthy type to be green?

96

Feel like you are Alice, living behind the looking glass— except that what you see is not quite Wonderland? Take a real looking glass with you wherever you go, and when someone says something absurd, simply take out your mirror and turn it toward the foolish one. If you are questioned about your actions, ask if they can draw a rectangle while staring into a mirror. You are now free to move on without repercussions—that mirror trick should keep them busy for a few hours.

97

Instead of categorizing shoes according to color, designer, or heel height, divide shoes up by length of time you can actually walk in them. Ten-minute shoes are great for those red carpet and award-presentation appearances, whereas ten-hour shoes are great for a day of shopping with second-cousin Bernice. In fact, you should think about giving those shoes to second-cousin Bernice.

98

No thoughtful query deserves the response, "Google it." That is just a lazy way of saying, "I don't have time for your silly, bothersome, insignificant question." If you cannot answer a sincere question with a quick sentence or two, perhaps you are not really an erudite intellectual. Now Google any words or phrases in the

preceding sentences that caused
you to wrinkle your brow.

99

Tell the small-talk-challenged
guests you're psychic, and watch
what happens! Give free holiday
readings to all partygoers. No,
you don't have to really be
psychic. You can usually say
something like, "You've been
somewhat frustrated by your
work and feel that if given the
chance, you could bring quite a
bit more creativity into the
mix." Or you could knowingly
nod and say, "People don't
always know how thoughtful
you really are, do they?"

100

When asked for your address,
always offer to give your
travelling friend a hint about
directions, roads, and points of
interest. Despite the ease of the

ubiquitous GPS device, it just might serve you to know the names of the major streets in your neighborhood or borough. And, why not take a trip that doesn't involve receiving turn-by-turn directions? Turn off the navigation function and unfold a vintage roadmap; find out if you really know how to find your way back home.

101

When making plans, treat all friends as if they might be the companion/date/love of your life. You most certainly would not rearrange a first date with your dreamy lover for a last-minute, seemingly better opportunity with your co-worker's mother-in-law, would you? Just use the same ladylike/gentlemanly ways with your friends as with your dates, and you will always have numerous pals fighting to be first on all of your guest lists.

102

Is a loud-mouthed cell phone user at the gym, grocery store, or hair salon disturbing you with her neurotic conversation and poor syntax? Quiet the annoying talker by boldly entering into the conversation. Supply witty and helpful retorts to anything you hear, and watch how quickly the talker lowers her volume, or—even better— puts the phone into your hands so you can argue her case.

103

Overwhelmed by facts from one side and fantasy from the other? Get into your personal Dewey Decimal mode, and think of it all as a trip to the library, the bookstore, or Amazon. Use your instincts to label one as fiction, the other as nonfiction. Do not be afraid to judge one as good and the other as bad. If we did not make

judgment calls, then how
would we know trash from the
truly chic, diamonds from
colored glass, or cream from
nonfat milk?

104

When faced with people who
do not agree with you on
political issues, state your point,
followed by this phrase: "I'm
Jodi Adler, and I approved this
message." A reminder, darlings:
you will want to use your own
name when putting this phrase
to use. If you are dealing with
the politically deaf, do not
bother trying to reason with
them; just treat them like the
toddlers they are—give them
a big hug, and suggest a nap.
Then pray that they forget
to vote.

105

If the enormity of a particular project is giving you the blues, take the opportunity to put your current frame of mind to good use. Write lyrics for a melancholy love song, ballad, or jazzy wail. Find a musician, and post the tune on a pay-for-play site—not only will you be making some money with your creative gloominess, you'll probably become a viral superstar with a huge book deal, and all the most attractive people will want to be your friends . . . though you'll now have another career/project to worry about.

106

Find out that some of the people in your inner circle have issues correctly citing your bon mots, retorts, and opinions? Keep a pocket-pack of Q-tips at the ready, and when handing

them out to your misquoting
companions, suggest they clean
that nasty wax out of their
ears—as you permanently clean,
delete, or fire-bomb these folk
off of your contacts list.

107

Does the help have the night
off? Auntie is not at all helpless
in the kitchen, and here's a hint:
neither are you. Use your
creative flair to create a one-
of-a kind dinner. Tonight's
inspiration: ratatouille. Let them
all think that you can't tell a
ramekin from a radish . . . and
then surprise everyone, because
as with your life, your cooking
adventures really don't require
a recipe.

108

When faced with a conversation
manipulator who uses the
phrases such as "you agree

that," or "you can see why we need to do this," remember that you can stop this amateur psycho-babbler in his or her tracks with the simple response, "No, not really." Remember to smile and keep a quizzical expression on your face, while holding fast to those three words of polite disagreement. You will always win your point—especially when you hold tight to the reality of the situation.

109

Feel like telling a dinner guest that they left clear-thinking logic in some cloudy situation room? Become a dinnertime diplomat, and smile as they spew their incredible nonsense. Answer back with a few wacky true facts, and before renewing the friendship or issuing another invitation, make a formal request for their visas the next time they attempt to cross the threshold into your home. It is just good policy, n'est-ce pas?

110

Are those anger management classes failing to ease the ongoing friction at home? Learn to properly channel that desire to slap, punch, or throttle your dear ones by taking to the stage at a local comedy club's open mic night, then watch as your fan base explodes. Be ready to sign with one of the top agents, who will find you just the right script—and transform you into the funniest, most highly paid, cutting-edge comic on the planet.

111

Not sure how to vote on any of those heavily skewed ballot measures, propositions, and popularity contests? Auntie does not like to get political—

but will share her one and only
secret to success in the voting
booth: Check your opponent's
ballot choices, then simply vote
the opposite way.

112

Worried about finances and
your future? Join legions of
fundraisers, and start your own
political action committee; or
perhaps you might start a
charity in your name, as many
athletes have done. If you are
worried about government
intervention and regulations,
just think positive thoughts—
and voilà, all those pesky rules
disappear. Add a personal touch
by sending out "Thank you for
your contribution" cards within
a week of any monetary deposit.
It is still important to be polite,
especially if you are writing
from inside a prison cell.

113

Darling, when you talk to Ms.
Friend about Auntie or anyone
else, you put Ms. Friend into a
very precarious position . . . it's
called gossip, or lashon hara—
and yes, my sweet, it is a sin.
Make sure you have your facts
straight—in every aspect of
your life—before you talk about
someone. (Unless of course you
are a writer of fiction. Then
write it all down, and give
Auntie a formal dedication,
kudos, or credit as your muse.
Also remember her in that all-
important residual stream,
in perpetuity.)

114

When relaying stories to a
friend, dinner companion, or
large crowd, remember to insert
the phrase "spoiler alert" every
so often. Not only does it draw
in the multitasker or technology
geek, it also gives your story an

extra bit of cachet—which will cause your tale to be repeated just often enough for you to become an internet legend.

115

Bored or overwhelmed with facts, figures, and poll results? Ignore the so-called experts, and start your own polling firm, so you may query the masses about life's really important and meaningful questions. Always remember to start by delving into an acquaintance's insights about you—it is nice to have the honest statistics about your true intelligence, grace, beauty, and wit close at hand. These are quite helpful for quick reference during those rare moments of self-doubt.

116

When Auntie was growing up, we all learned how to be

gracious winners and losers, though it seems that this sort of instruction has skipped a generation—or two. Some dear dolts must now be taught what it means to be a gracious winner or to—gasp—lose at a competitive event. This means that you must not boast, gloat, or rub your foe's nose in their loss—doing such a thing makes you the ultimate loser. Auntie believes friendship is a greater gift than any passing victory.

117

If you should find yourself stuck in conversation with a dear soul who will not let you leave—asking yet another leading question, hanging on your arm, or using your kindness as a means of avoiding their particular brand of weekly anonymous meeting—quickly end the tête-à-tête by placing your fist to your chest while uttering the actors' saving grace,

"and, **scene**." After bowing,
you are now free turn on your
heel and head for the bar.

118

See someone walking down the
boulevard in a getup that begs
for a major intervention? Be
generous with your knowledge
of color, texture, and fashion.
Offer to donate your time to
become their personal stylist.
Not only will you be able to
shop without having to foot the
bill, you will also be doing a
service for all mankind—while
overseeing a Pygmalion-like
change in a grateful soul.

119

Find that your phone calls
are not being returned, your
text messages are being missed,
or you've been dropped,
perhaps even un-friended, by an
acquaintance or long-time pal?

No need to worry yourself
about this ungrateful lout: if
anyone leaves your inner circle
without explanation, they need
to look long and hard into a
mirror. Only a coward leaves a
relationship, soirée, or
government appointment
without at least a nod, a
handshake, or the filing of
a formal complaint.

120

Is a needy acquaintance
continually reminding you that
your offhand/spot-on
comments are being taken—
ahem—"personally"? Auntie
knows that a dear one's
unresolved family issues always
make for some hideously
tiresome exchanges. Suggest
that this over-sensitive soul
stop making every matter,
from holiday table seating
assignments to best-selling book
reviews and theater critiques, a
topic of blathering debate.

However, if the need for a lethal
duel develops—then by all
means, sharpen your blade
and plunge it in.

121

Tired of the everyday misuse
and overuse of crass language
and swear words? Thumb
through a dictionary, and
increase your vocabulary while
you upscale your list of insults.
Use classic and archaic words to
ever-so-politely insult the idiots
in your midst. Among my
favorites: battleaxe, mooncalf,
harridan, virago, ninny hammer,
and harpy.

122

Really, my darlings, if you have
anything of value to add to
our conversation, by all means,
say it aloud—so we can all
appreciate your wit, opinion, or
idiocy. Mumbling responses are

for nitwits, cowards, and dullards … so do us all a favor, and keep that mumbling to yourself.

123

At a party with a bunch of sincere, naïve and incredibly dull do-gooders? Do your own good deed, and disagree (always politely) with every opinion or cause they stubbornly adhere/cling to. Keep disagreeing until the conversation becomes laughingly silly, ridiculous, or you find the inspiration for your next screenplay. Just for fun, give a conspiratorial wink to the unwitting leader of the opposition as you exit the salon.

124

The next time someone tells you of their grand and glorious plans for their career, marriage,

spouse, or children, don't try to
tell them they are living in a
fantasy world or lying to
themselves. Simply nod, and
offer up a bit of true fantasy
philosophy, such as "you only
succeed if your undies are
inside-out," or "never use
a knife when you can use a
spoon." They will undoubtedly
believe you.

125

Auntie abhors all things smug.
There really is no reason for this
point of view. It is obnoxious,
pretentious, and unkind. Smug
seems to be the worst variety of
that falsely superior attitude so
many people have assumed
these days, due to their lack of
graciousness. If you should
happen to meet someone who
is condescendingly smug, simply
remember your own
upbringing, your sense of
noblesse oblige—and then attack
the smug one with anything

nearby that has a sharp edge—
preferably your own brain.

126

Have you recently discovered a
small group of evil, envious
leeches has sneaked into your
world? If you were not so
fabulously funny, gorgeous,
smart, witty, wealthy, polite,
successful, endearingly nice,
charitable, and sexy . . . those
people would have nothing to
talk about. Excise the poor
souls from your life by hiring
them as assistants, having them
sign nondisclosure agreements,
sending them off on some wild
errands . . . and then taking
notes for your next best-seller
as they attempt to get some real
work done.

127

Do you have friends with
habitual tardiness issues? Start

keeping track of their on-time record, so that you might compare their numbers with your least favorite airline's on-time stats. Politely bring this up after their lateness record surpasses the airline's (have charts and documentation at the ready). Then request an upgrade to First Class, which in this case means a downgrade in any future invitations sent to these self-involved, egocentric, arrogant folk.

128

Does every family get-together become a real life episode of the game show Family Feud? Why not make this year's reunion pay off—for at least one branch of your family tree? Evenly divide the group, and then go around the table, asking prepared questions of all the attendees. Turn up the fun by providing everyone with a noisemaker/ buzzer so that no whispering or cheating can occur without being called out. Provide a cash payout—a small annuity works best—to the winning side. Assign the losers to KP duty.

129

Auntie would like to share a secret she learned from her dear Daddy: If you should be involved in an argument or lawsuit, and the other side concedes a point . . . stop and acknowledge your win, and then move on to your next point. Continuing to argue further, to prove how wrong or idiotic your foe is, will not help you in any way. It may even cause additional irrational, non-winnable points to be conjured up.

130

Want permission to poke your nose into everyone's business at will? Simply attach the word "Consultant" to your name, and head out into the world. Catch the image of someone who needs a neck lift or nose job? Use tact while offering beauty tips as a Cosmetic Surgery Consultant. Spy a basket at the grocer's full of all the wrong kinds of foodstuffs? Toss a few dining tips to the shopper—now you're a Nutritional Consultant. See an overzealous amateur designer wearing too many floral prints? Quickly end that trend in your capacity as a Clothing Consultant. Be kind and gentle when offering all this free advice—remember, not everyone will appreciate your wise and knowing eye.

131

Has the owner of a home with not-so-clean carpets asked you to remove your shoes before crossing the threshold into her lovely abode? Unless this is a well-known ethnic/family custom that would throw the embassy's protocol minister into a tizzy, you are allowed to politely ignore this request while keeping your tootsies inside your shoes. When inviting a guest into your home, the idea is to make them feel welcome— not immediately ask them to disrobe. Unless, of course, it is a disrobing kind of party—and in that case, bring plenty of disinfectant.

132

Fascinated by a pop-culture topic that is intriguing or headline-ready? Before gathering facts or investigating the root of the issue, invite a

group of friends to start a
discussion group, and offer to
lead—as a charity organizer.
Watch in amazement as dozens
of extra souls beg to join in
"for the cause."

133

It is always fun to get an
unexpected gift—and a
thoughtful, anonymous present
to someone who actually needs
something can be kind and
caring. Know someone full of
hot air? Tastefully wrap up a
bottle of Beano and send it
overnight express. Remember, it
is immature to always need
recognition for your good
deeds, so do not worry about
getting a thank-you note.

134

Surrounded by the PC police?
Want to have a private giggle?
Ask the PC officer why he or

she has those beliefs. Scratch your head, wrinkle up your nose, or just act confused. Remember to always be polite when posing your query. Give them 30 seconds to explain. Of course, this works best if you have a second hand on your watch or a timer app on your phone. Shout, "GO!" when the official timing begins. GO!

135

Whispering fools talking about you across the table at a dinner party? Laughingly instruct these rude plebeians that a hand positioned in front of the mouth with a searing gaze in anyone's direction is the epitome of gauche. Then demonstrate using a stage *sotto voce* tone, saying things such as "that woman with the ugly haircut steals from her boss," or "she abused her first ex-husband." Remember to summon your driver to bring

the car around before the next
round of rumors begins.

136

Find yourself trying to connect
the dots, only to end up with
false positives, stale gossip, and
bits of misinformation about
everything? Auntie finds it
increasingly amusing that people
jump to outrageous conclusions
about all sorts of things simply
because of the way someone
looks, their political affiliation,
or their zip code. Leave the real
sleuthing to the nation's
spooks—so you are free to
go back to reading the latest
romance or thriller, while
chatting about matters of
greater importance—such
as Grace's bad hair color
or boob job.

137

Are nametags being doled out at a soirée or premiere? Have a bit of fun, and use a *nom de party* for that sticky little piece of paper. If another moniker does not immediately come to mind, simply write in the name of a little-known author, silent film star, or jazz musician. Personal favorites include Nellie Bly, Pola Negri, and June Christy.

138

Is there an overly zealous do-gooder in your life who is trying to get you to a team-building exercise, a log cabin retreat, a hand-holding "share" session, or an icebreaker for some darling new charity? Inform the altruistic one that you only team up with those you personally deem worthy, you will gladly retreat to a log cabin if there is room service, and that you gladly welcome all icebreakers

that are accompanied by a
glass —and some lovely
vodka and tonic.

139

Auntie is seeing quite a bit of
stone-throwing these days, and
would like to remind you
darlings that despite your quick
wit and mighty strength . . .
your houses . . . they are still
made of glass. Hard to believe,
is it not? Only throw stones if
your own house is properly
secured—or if you no longer
want to be in contact with
your victims.

140

Darlings, if you are going to
make an attempt at a humorous
retort, make sure your response
does not need to be *explained* to
your audience. We all know that
the only possible result of such

clarification will be an
embarrassingly loud thud.

141

Some people are off-beat;
others are simply insane. It can
be loads of fun to be around
either group—the trick is to
escape from the relationship
before the insane begin to take
themselves at their own word.

142

If you're supplying advice,
counsel, or a shoulder to
cry on to many a friend or
acquaintance, then it's high
time you start calling yourself
a Coach. There are so many
options out there: Life Couch,
Dating Coach, Investment
Coach, Find-Your-Life-Passion
Coach. Just print up some
business cards, and go for it.
Chances are you know many a
soul with fancy letters tagging

along after their names—and in comparison, your advice will, most likely, be much more valuable and heartfelt.

143

Despite your skills and knowledge, Auntie is requesting that you resist the urge to correct the minor (and major) grammatical errors you see in friends' writing—unless, of course, you are an English professor or grammar guru. Is it not more important to know that your friend has something special to tell you? Auntie is disconcerted by each and every grammatical error as much as (if not more than) thou art—but she knows that the power of friendship always trumps the proper placement of an apostrophe, comma, or participle.

144

Don't be one of those who
proclaim that "I'm not into
funerals." Few really are, unless
you are a member of the
walking dead. That, darling,
is not what funerals are about.
We go to funerals for all sorts
of reasons: because we loved
someone or because they
meant something to us, or, as
they say, "to pay our respects."
Remember—if you cannot
grant respect, you certainly
won't command it.

145

Know someone who takes
more than the proverbial mile
when nary an inch is offered?
With this sort, it is best to rein
in all offers at all times. To
counter their misuse and
manipulation of your thought-
fulness, immediately end all
interaction—there is never a
middle ground with those who

fail to appreciate our sincere help and kind efforts.

146

When catching someone in a lie, the issue is not necessarily the lie itself, but rather this: it is a guaranteed bet that this poor soul will indeed lie again. To counteract any such future problems with the delusional person, suggest that he or she write down all responses to any query of yours. Do not waste their creativity—simply sign them up as a writing partner, making sure your contract is the best boilerplate you can find.

147

If you ever want to incite Auntie to riot, simply tell her to "just calm down." Is there another seemingly innocuous phrase that is so very frustrating to hear? What you are seeing is

Auntie's version of calm. Now
go calm down yourselves,
darlings.

148

Feeling overwhelmed, but don't
feel that any self-help program
is a good fit for your particular
issue? Start your own 12-Step
program, counseling group, or
religion. Invite all of your
clients and friends to the initial
meeting, and then watch as
your personal popularity soars.
Having an entourage always
provides an immediate boost to
one's self-esteem.

149

Auntie wants to remind her dear
friends that we may nod and
listen to your tale of woe the
first two, three, or four times.
We may even appear to hang on
every word, as you retell your
story of a personal world gone

mad . . . but in reality, our responses are simply the result of a good upbringing. Your job, dear one, is to look up the meaning of the word "discretion." Shut down your self-serving urge to tell us your sordid story one more time, especially if we should ever again cross paths.

150

Are you fighting the urge to spew vile words about some ex-lover, former boss, or erstwhile friend? Unless the information is of a caliber that would entice the editors of TMZ or some such organization, save yourself from public humiliation or a lawsuit: Change the players' names, and write down all the juicy little tidbits for inclusion in your upcoming novella. You must however, pinky swear that you will remember to call Auntie and share all the really

sordid details before the first
edition is released.

151

Yes, darlings, you can fix some
things on your own—and be
entrepreneurial at the same
time. Auntie Jodi is so proud of
herself: while trouble-shooting a
computer problem all by
herself, she was amazed that she
could fix the issue. If plugging
in all those look-alike black
wires takes an engineering
degree, Auntie now has a Ph.D.
She is setting up an online
degree program of her own,
with diplomas that are tastefully
designed. Take note that all
diplomas will be sent out as
soon as the enrollment fees are
paid—in full.

152

When discussing the popularity
of movies, media-types, and

moguls, let your tablemates
dither on for as long as possible
before letting them all know
that your personal approval
rating is the highest it has been
in seven years. Smile as you
inquire into their untallied
totals—sipping on a good
Cabernet always helps to ease
the tedium of their responses.

153

Auntie knows that revenge is
best served cold. In fact, Auntie
serves her revenge so very cold,
it is politely offered up in a
goblet that has been stored in
the freezer for a year or two,
with a hearty serving of icy
shards in the mix. Just enough
to turn your lips arctic blue,
but not quite cold enough
to induce instant death.

WINTER

154

If you should find yourself waking up on your hosts' settee after celebrating with them, always remember to leave a small gratuity tucked under a nearby knickknack. Depending on the accommodations, it is customary to leave between $2 and $7 per night. If you only have large bills, do not ask for change.

155

If you should be seated at a dinner party next to a know-it-all who in reality knows very little, begin your conversation with the following phrase: "Nine out of ten people surveyed agree with the idea that . . . " It does not matter if no one agrees with you, and it does not matter if you are telling the truth. Just remember to use that simple phrase, because no one checks facts these days.

156

No, darlings, that comment you overheard was not at all mean: it was simply the unvarnished truth, offered without an ounce of malice. Indeed, it was witty and sharp and honest. Simply learn to connect the dots as presented to you in life. One day, you just might be able to accept the picture that

ultimately reveals itself. You
may also want to discuss
your issues with your shrink,
sponsor, or self-esteem coach.

157

Make your own "Naughty or
Nice" list, but keep the
requirements for inclusion a
secret. At your next holiday
party, hand out symbolic gifts
or favors to each guest, while
announcing that each item has
special significance to each
recipient. If a certain person
needs to be taught a lesson,
make that gift a sly statement of
thinly-veiled truth. When
dealing with the dense—or the
sensitive—it might be best to
refrain from signing the "From"
portion of the gift tag.

158

Darlings, we are *all* long-
distance calls—so please find

another excuse when you accidently pick up our call. Have a few well-rehearsed, less common reasons for cutting the conversation short—perhaps you and your personal chef are planning vegan appetizers, or maybe you are signing a lucrative charity endorsement deal. Saying you are on a long-distance call is so very ho-hum, 1970s, and rude.

159

Telling us the story of your teenage daughter's coming-of-age definitely qualifies you as an oversharing mother—even if you are doing so on a cleverly hidden internet site. Would you tell this story at a State Dinner, or while accepting a nationally recognized award? If not, then save the share for your personal diaries. By withholding this information, you are not only salvaging many a friendship—you are also saving your child from permanent humiliation, and the need for additional counseling. In this case, it is indeed the mother's fault. Of course, if the share is truly unique, we just might be able to get you a two-picture deal.

160

Have you encountered a clerk or customer service rep with an unnaturally high, fake, sweet, little-girl voice? When asked, "How can I help you?" simply request that the dear clerk lower her voice by at least an octave. If this is not possible, start responding in kind—using your best squeaky-pitched falsetto until the call or encounter ends. This provides you with great practice, too; that way you will be ready when called upon for a last-minute recasting of Minnie Mouse in an animated special.

161

Always have a short acceptance speech at the ready for those unexpected moments when you are awarded a seemingly out-of-the-blue accolade for your civic, artistic, or creative endeavors. You never know when a statuette will be thrust into your hands, with the spotlight on. Remember to be gracious, and when thanking all those who helped along the way, always take the high road—saving the inside jokes and sniping for another day.

162

Here's a practical little reminder: just as the bread plate goes to your left, while your drink goes to your right, your current beau should always be within arm's length, while his ex-wives and former girlfriends should always be in another zip code.

163

Are you sleep-deprived with a calendar full of must-do engagements? Pretend you are jet-lagged. Regale the crowd with stories of your latest cross-continental romp as you struggle to keep your head from bobbing back while losing consciousness. Chances are, your tales of adventure will become even more interesting as the crowd watches you trail off to sleep mid-sentence.

164

Clueless cad or greedy gal issue invites to his/her "no host" birthday party at a local hot spot? Be careful if you should decide to attend this soiree. Auntie always errs on the side of generosity, but more often than not, we generous attendees end up footing more than our fair share of the tacky host's and cheap guests' bill. Bring a limited number of greenbacks. Be generous when tipping the help, but do not allow yourself to be guilt-tripped into paying for the cheapskates in your midst. In fact, this just might be the only time you'll want to discreetly ask for a separate check.

165

What type of cotillion does one graduate from that allows the diner to rest his or her non-dominant arm on the dining table while shoveling food into the mouth with the wrong fork? It's not breeding, darlings—anyone who wants to learn can do so. We all know about keeping elbows off the table; that goes for forearms, too.

166

Give yourself a title. No, not the usual Mr., Miss, Mrs., or Dr.—

rather, something that aligns with your current frame of mind, skills, or interests. I personally know a Mayor of Awesomeville, a Prince of Impolite Banter, a Queen of Parallel Parking, the General Contractor to all of Beverly Hills, and of course the Baron of Cheap Cabernets. How would you like to be addressed?

167

Should you be on the road and distressed about another driver's actions, make sure your toddler has earplugs firmly planted in his sweet little ears before you launch into a vulgar, profane, and tired tirade. It is true: one day, when you least expect it, your child will surprise you with his stupendous four-letter word recall skills.

168

Auntie could do without the
term "bucket list." It is such a
silly phrase; why not do all the
fun, interesting things you'd like
to do, and make it part of your
everyday life? A true adventure
is much more mysterious to the
outside world when treated
modestly—as an offhand,
everyday escapade. I'd bet that
HRH Elizabeth II doesn't have
a bucket list. You don't need
one, either. Perform your deed,
and then regale us with your tale
while sipping prosecco.

169

Auntie has no idea why any man
would want to take his wife's
name. What a silly, backward,
anti-femme idea. Perhaps
Auntie should say that she
would never become the wife of
a man who wanted to take her
name. That is just a backward
world. Evidence for Auntie's

side: How many teen boys doodled their names enmeshed with their crushes' names, while pretending to calculate a cosine and tangent? Now . . . you do the math.

170

Is a humorless, suffering soul forcing you to explain or justify your every witticism, bon mot, or good mood? Politely free yourself from the tyranny of that friendship; as a parting gift, offer the names of some self-help groups, medications, or cocktail recipes. Someday, he or she may realize that we well adjusted folk have feelings, too.

171

Is there a crazy person following you around— emailing, ranting, unable to see the error of her ways? Become a sweet Southern belle for a moment, and respond to her with the ever-so-passively polite "bless your heart." Watch the craziness escalate . . . and, voilà!—the next chapter of your thriller is quickly completed.

172

Here's an easy way to get rid of those hangers-on. Keep a mini voodoo paper doll (easily made using an old photo or free-hand drawing) in your purse or shirt pocket; and when the pesky person comes a bit too near, simply start sticking the voodoo paper doll with anything sharp that happens to be nearby. Not only will you keep the evil vibes away, it makes for a great conversation starter with the nice folks who are already seated around you.

173

Darlings, just because you have something to add to a scintillating conversation does *not* mean that you need to weigh in right this second. Might I suggest that you listen in for a few moments before sharing your *non sequitur?* Discretion is, indeed, often the better part of conversational valor.

174

Are things not going quite your way in your job, relationship, or family reunion? Just start issuing your personal brand of executive orders—it does not matter if anyone adheres to any of your edicts, and it does not matter if your orders are ethical. Ultimately, you will feel better—and we all know that it is simply about you, and only you. No one else really matters. Except Auntie, of course.

175

No matter what language you speak, smug never translates into funny. Unless, of course, you are performing for an audience of one.

176

When on a blind date, if you should find yourself stuck in conversation with a clueless, bullying, arrogant-for-no-good-reason bore, use this interaction as a means of looking at how those without moral fiber behave. Innocently interview and prod. If you should inadvertently anger this damaged creature, take thorough mental notes for a character in your next best-selling murder mystery. Chances are you will never again encounter such an uncivil lout in your life. Remember; never let a rude soul steal anything from your gracious heart.

177

Auntie Jodi wants you to realize that your public and private group posts give us huge clues about your likes, dislikes, successes, failures, kinks, Achilles heels, and ever so much more. Do you really want all of us to know? We are more than able to connect the dots; obviously, your unconscious brain is unable to do so. Once read, these things are never unread. Perhaps a bit of self-editing might be in order.

178

When in public, if you should be engaged in a mad, passionate, or achingly sweet embrace or kiss, be sure to slyly check for surveillance cameras, drones, or snoopy neighbors. Privacy, as we knew it just a few years ago, no longer exists. However, if you should be lucky enough to observe a high-profile A-lister in such a situation it's best to snap your photos quickly—so that you can be first in line to collect a high finder's fee from a tabloid, website, or government agency.

179

If you should find yourself in the company of a nonstop nonsense talker, simply press your personal Mute button on a seen or unseen pocket-sized remote control. Any electronic device, real or imagined, can be used for this purpose. Simply aim your real or mimed device at the inane chatter-box while saying, "click, click" out loud. With the dear soul on silent, you no longer have to respond or feign interest—just smile and nod while thinking about your growing bank account, an upcoming vacation, or your unerring sense of style.

180

After responding in the
affirmative, should you find
yourself feeling less than
enthusiastic about attending a
party, concert, inauguration, or
coronation, always send a
personal note of regret—or,
if need be, make a quick, last-
minute phone call . . . explaining
yourself to your hosts. Asking a
friend who is attending to relay
your message of incapacitation
is not only rude, it is also
positively dreary and oh-so-
very-high school.

181

Has your lighthearted point of
view caused some dreary dullard
to tell you to "grow up"? Never
ever allow those unimaginative
ones to degrade your *joie de vivre*,
and darlings—be brave enough
to only grow up in the areas of
your life wherein it is *absolutely*
necessary.

182

Is that PC-sanctioned list of banned products, people, ideas, and programs growing by those proverbial leaps and bounds? Start your own list of The Banned. At the top of your list, place the people who compose those ridiculous proscriptions. One must refuse to be around the ignorant, the humorless, the controlling, and the unimaginative. Do not let them box you in—or out. Always be your fabulously unique self.

183

Instantly increase your personal cachet: simply place an initial in front of your first name. Try it for a few days and see what happens. And just call me Auntie Z. Jodi.

184

Auntie does not believe in
burning bridges; however,
it may sometimes become
necessary to verbally singe a few
edges as you gracefully exit
from an unfriendly or unkind
work, personal, or online
environment.

185

Do you need to sound a bit
more highbrow around some
pretentious companions? Think
quickly, and hyphenate your last
name—or use a surname as
a first name. Try using well-
known artists' names or titles,
such as Lord, Baron, Von, and
Smith. I shall temporarily be
known as Adler Baron
Hockney-Smith.

186

Auntie wants you to know that disagreement does not equate to being evil, stupid, or mean. If we disagree, and you present logical, sensible arguments for your point, you just might earn our respect. Name-calling, however, especially in lieu of civil discourse, is a waste of Auntie's time.

187

Auntie would like to request that if you have children, you assume the role of parent *at all times* until each child is 18 or of sound mind (that condition may require an additional decade). Just because something is cute, trendy, or funny does not make the behavior welcome in restaurants, or houses of worship—or, for that matter, in any public forum.

188

Auntie would never suggest
that anyone hold back from
speaking from the heart.
Despite some oft-cited rules of
polite society, being opinionated
is much preferred to leading a
common, fearful, milquetoast
life. However, it may sometimes
be prudent to hold back from
stating your point of view in
order to see where some newly
made friends—perhaps, soon-
to-be sworn enemies—actually
do stand.

189

No, darlings, there never will
come a time when the phrase
"boys will be boys" ceases being
useful. Instead of complaining,
simply respect men for the
creatures they are—and then
calculate the number of coven
members required for your
spells to take effect.

190

If you feel the need to brag
about your career, children,
spouse, book deal, weight loss,
income stream, sexual
conquests, or other such
subject, survey your audience
before launching into your spiel.
Chances are that you, dear soul,
are the only one who is truly
interested. Yawn.

191

Darlings, if you cannot speak on
the telephone, do not pick up
and tell the caller that "I can't
talk right now." This is what
caller I.D. and voicemail are all
about. Is there anything as
annoying as having someone
answer the phone, only to tell
you that they can't answer the
phone? If you have no time
for a polite "Hello," avoid all
misunderstandings and hurt
feelings by simply ignoring the
call entirely. This way, you

avoid looking like a rude,
self-centered, phone-
addicted luddite.

192

While on your commute to
work, should you find yourself
weeping uncontrollably, getting
lost *en route*, or plotting the
murder of your boss, it may be
time to consider a career
change. Your dramatic exit
from the wretched work
environment will be a welcome
diversion for your soon-to-be
ex-colleagues.

193

If you should find yourself
being underappreciated by
anyone, at any time, it is best
to immediately cut ties to the
useless oaf. Why on Earth
would you ever spend a single
second of your life among those
who are not grateful to be in

your presence, and are unaware
of your obvious charms? And
please don't tell Auntie it is a
self-esteem issue.

194

Do not make Auntie listen to
groups of allegedly talented,
cute, precocious children
singing in a group. No amount
of champagne can soften their
tones to something close to a
tenor or baritone range, and
earplugs, as useful as they are,
will never be considered chic.

195

Caught in conversation with a
self-absorbed chatterbox who is
unaware that conversation does
not mean monologue? Since she
is so very rude, be exceptionally
polite as you brazenly interrupt
the blathering soul with a *non
sequitur* such as, "I'm doing
splendidly, thank you for
118

asking." Then shake the dear one's hand as you smile, raise an eyebrow and commandeer the conversation away. Fire with fire, darlings.

196

Find yourself surrounded by phonies who do not know that they are fake, ersatz, or plastic beyond compare? Simply flash these poor souls your most sincere smile, while offering up a few shocking truths . . . along the lines of "your socioeconomic status belies your true lack of finesse," or "your darling mama wears bottes d'armée." No need to worry about offending these souls—it's all in good fun, isn't it?

197

Sending good wishes to all during the holidays is a welcome

change from the nasty-spewing evil-eyed sentiments that are too often sent out during non-holiday times. Auntie knows you are just trying to be polite, but inserting that qualifying phrase, "to all those who celebrate," is overly careful. Throw caution to the wind, and sincerely heap good cheer of all sorts on everyone. We all need as many good thoughts as possible these days.

198

Are you dealing with a tedious dear one who claims, "I never drink alone"? Have pity on the poor dear and offer to show her how—while in her company, pour out a single vodka martini, and sip on it while conversing with her. Not only will you have made your point, you will have survived a chat that might otherwise have been deadly dull—had you lacked the foresight to drink alone.

199

Have a Queen with a bee in
his or her bonnet making
unnecessarily nasty remarks
about your lovely, happiness-
filled life? Answer all comments
without guile, but with a big
grin—as you patiently wait for
an answer from this envious
soul. Chances are, you will be
waiting a very long time.

200

If you're feeling a bit restless at
your next celebration, offer to
take other guests on the Royal
Tour of the house or apartment.
Yes, this can be on your first
visit to the abode. Walk around
the entire place, pointing out
interesting paintings or pieces
of furniture in each room. Use
your best tour guide voice, and
when noting items of interest,
remember to ask guests for a
thumbs-up or thumbs-down
regarding the décor.

201

If you smile at your fellow party-goers, they'll probably smile back; some might even amble over to chat. Unless, of course, everyone is wearing black and is just too cool for the room. In that case, pretend you are Wednesday Addams, and skulk around . . . you'll be very popular. Merry Merry!

202

Hate small talk? Bring up politics, and as soon as you find two people with differing opinions, bring them together. If they refuse to hold hands while singing "We Are the World," offer to moderate a debate between them. Give them ten minutes to prep. This works really well if relatives are involved.

203

Lovelorn and left out on
Valentine's Day? Just pick up
a box of children's themed
cards, and play Cupid while
handing them out to people
you encounter during the day.
Do not worry about true love
pairings; divorce solves all those
messy mistakes. Sign the cards
with a flourish, adding few x's
and o's and making sure you
save the best card for your
current crush. Ladies, seal
the deal with a red lipstick
"SWAK" impression on the
back of the envelope.

204

Feeling as if you give, and
give, and give again, yet no
one seems to realize or
recognize you for your efforts?
Remember, darling, charity does
indeed begin at home, so be
charitable to yourself once in a
while. After giving to Sissy and

Cousin Jasper, remember to give yourself something—even if it's just a pat on the back or a glass of really yummy prosecco. How can you possibly continue to help others if you do not help yourself?

www.ingramcontent.com/pod-product-compliance
Lightning Source LLC
Chambersburg PA
CBHW061956040426
42447CB00010B/1780